MEN ON THE VERGE OF A HIS-PANIC BREAKDOWN

A Play in Monologues
by
GUILLERMO REYES

Dramatic Publishing
Woodstock, Illinois • London, England • Melbourne, Australia

*** NOTICE ***

The amateur and stock acting rights to this work are controlled exclusively by THE DRAMATIC PUBLISHING COMPANY without whose permission in writing no performance of it may be given. Royalty fees are given in our current catalog and are subject to change without notice. Royalty must be paid every time a play is performed whether or not it is presented for profit and whether or not admission is charged. A play is performed any time it is acted before an audience. All inquiries concerning amateur and stock rights should be addressed to:

DRAMATIC PUBLISHING
P. O. Box 129, Woodstock, Illinois 60098

COPYRIGHT LAW GIVES THE AUTHOR OR THE AUTHOR'S AGENT *THE EXCLUSIVE RIGHT TO MAKE COPIES.* This law provides authors with a fair return for their creative efforts. Authors earn their living from the royalties they receive from book sales and from the performance of their work. Conscientious observance of copyright law is not only ethical, it encourages authors to continue their creative work. This work is fully protected by copyright. No alterations, deletions or substitutions may be made in the work without the prior written consent of the publisher. No part of this work may be reproduced or transmitted in any form or by any means, electronic or mechanical, including photocopy, recording, videotape, film, or any information storage and retrieval system, without permission in writing from the publisher. It may not be performed either by professionals or amateurs without payment of royalty. All rights, including but not limited to the professional, motion picture, radio, television, videotape, foreign language, tabloid, recitation, lecturing, publication, and reading are reserved.

For performance of any songs and recordings mentioned in this play which are in copyright, the permission of the copyright owners must be obtained or other songs and recordings in the public domain substituted.

©MCMXCIX by
GUILLERMO REYES

Printed in the United States of America
All Rights Reserved
(MEN ON THE VERGE OF A HIS-PANIC BREAKDOWN)

ISBN 0-87129-899-6

IMPORTANT BILLING AND CREDIT REQUIREMENTS

All producers of the Play *must* give credit to the Author(s) of the Play in all programs distributed in connection with performances of the Play and in all instances in which the title of the Play appears for purposes of advertising, publicizing or otherwise exploiting the Play and/or a production. The name of the Author(s) *must* also appear on a separate line, on which no other name appears, immediately following the title, and *must* appear in size of type not less than fifty percent the size of the title type. Biographical information on the author(s), if included in this book, may be used on all programs. *On all programs this notice must appear:*

"Produced by special arrangement with
THE DRAMATIC PUBLISHING COMPANY of Woodstock, Illinois"

PRODUCTION HISTORY

MEN ON THE VERGE OF A HIS-PANIC BREAKDOWN originally premiered in Los Angeles at the Celebration Theater, June 1994, starring Felix Pire. The production was directed by Joseph Megel. Set and costume design was by Leonard Pollack.

A subsequent production opened in San Francisco at the Theatre Rhinoceros, September 1994, starring George Castillo, directed by Joseph Megel. It also played at the City Lights Theatre in San Jose in the summer of 1995.

MEN ON THE VERGE OF A HIS-PANIC BREAKDOWN was produced off-Broadway in March 1997 by Playwrights Preview Productions/Francis Hill Associates at the 47th Street Playhouse, starring Felix Pire, and directed by Joseph Megel.

MEN ON THE VERGE OF A HIS-PANIC BREAKDOWN

A Series of Comedic Monologues

For 1 to 7 Men

Contents

Prologue	7
Scene One: The Gay Little Immigrant That Could	8
Scene Two: Good-bye to Sugar Daddy	13
Scene Three: Hispanically Correct	17
Scene Four: Demon Roommate From Hell	23
Scene Five: Federico Writes Again	29
Scene Six: Castro's Queen	32
Scene Seven: ESL: English as a Stressful Language	37
Scene Eight: Drag Flamenco	42
Epilogue: The Marriage of Federico	47

Running time: Approximately 1 hour, 40 minutes.
Simple unit set.

PROLOGUE

(All the props, costumes and furniture hang on a rack as if in an all-purpose bazaar of improbable pieces brought together. The table tops for the "Castro's Queen" monologue, for instance, look like giant Carmen Miranda hats, and yet when they're turned over and placed in a stool, they create a restaurant table.

The Man on the Verge enters as the music plays. He sees his set hanging up there. It's time to put on the show, to live out the fantasy, the laughter, the pathos, to do it all over again as if somewhere, in metaphysical space, he's destined to do this many times, preferably off-Broadway, but on the road as well, in a big theatre, or a small theatre anywhere on earth.

He takes down the T-shirt that he'll need for the first monologue, and the show's ready to start. Throughout the transitions, he'll continue to discard the props and take off the new ones until, by the end of the play, the stage will lay bare as if the truth has been spoken and stands there naked in space for the audience to see. The actor will not have left the stage, all the transitions and changes of costume will have been done in front of the audience in dim light and choreographed to the beat of the music.)

SCENE ONE:

THE GAY LITTLE IMMIGRANT THAT COULD

(FEDERICO: a young man, early 20s, thick accent.)

April 29, 1992

Querida Madre,
Dear Mother,

My first day in Los Angeles, and I already have everything I want.

I arrived with the address book in my hand full of possibilities, and phone numbers of potential wealthy backers... So I go, "Knock, knock, knock. Hello, it's me Federico. Remember me? You come to my country to help fight for social justice and help pick, ah, native fruits? You are courageous American student of native ways who say to me if ever I come to the United States of America, and experience openly gay lifestyle, you help me settle down, find a job, and introduce me to atmosphere rife with sexual openings." *(Blast!)* The door come shut on my face on my first attempt to fit into openly gay lifestyle.

But not to worry, Mamacita, I try again. Because I believe when you try and try again, doors open. That is the American way of life! You keep trying for that one door to open!

Men on the Verge of a His-panic Breakdown

I walk the streets of Los Angeles, and I for myself, see the excitement of the American lifestyle. I see fire and smoke in the horizon, and I say: "Oh, must be those Hollywood folk making another *Lethal Weapon* sequel!" People running, fire trucks rushing back and forth, policemen in riot gear hiding behind doughnut shops. And I see for myself that America lives up to its image in the movies. I hear a blast! I look around me, a drug store is on fire, people rush into a shoe store and pick out whatever they want! That is America, Mamá, such enthusiastic consumer appetite!

I go to my next address: "Knock, knock, it's me Federico. Remember me? You and I experienced compromising positions while you got away from your country to study fertility rituals among same-sex indigenous couples. Well, I come to experience openly gay lifestyle in your homeland." *(Blast!)*

The door comes shut on my face again, Mamacita. And one by one, doors shut on my face, and my potential wealthy backers forget all the promises they make when they come to my country to deflower native bottom like myself...

Well, I had one more address to go to. So I go... "Knock, knock, knock. I'm Federico. I am your pen pal. You write to me for the last five years and you say if ever I come to America, you help me settle down. You are financially stable man eager to meet men from my country willing to submit themselves to socioeconomic dependency. Well, here I am, gringuito. Make me your love slave!"

Of course, now I am standing on the entrance to this building, and I notice things very different from what he say in

Men on the Verge of a His-panic Breakdown

his letter. He is supposed to be handsome young man who work as a model, live in a neighborhood worthy of American prosperous lifestyle, so that we spend weekends together in Palm Springs sprinkling our seed through the desert. But here I am standing on the doorstep of his building—and there is a drunk man lying on the mat.

I am knocking on his door now, and the knocker falls off on my hand. I am beginning to suspect he is going through a recession... "Knock, knock, knock. Remember me? I'm Federico." Then the door open, and a wheelchair pop out, a blanket covering his feet, and a large pink toupee sticks out almost covering his face... and I tell him, "You are not the man I correspond with all these years. You don't live in prosperous economic indulgence. You are not model with tight chest, rippling biceps and solid wardrobe." And then he say—and this is where his voice turn deep and spooky, and the wind stirs the palm trees which are now on fire— he say, "Young man, curfew begins at sundown!" And I stand, oh, mesmerized. "Go home or the L.A.P.D. is gonna get ya!"

The L.A.P.D.—what deep meaning was held in such words? But people are running inside, shutting their doors, as the palm trees burn... "Riot," they shout. "Riot!" I begin to understand. There I stand in the hallway of my cockroach-infested American Dream.

I really have no more addresses or phone numbers to go to this time... Night begin to fall. People drive fast home, passing me by. "Curfew!" they shout, "Go home! Curfew!" And I say, "Ay, que curfew ni que na! In my coun-

Men on the Verge of a His-panic Breakdown

try curfew last fifteen years, curfew!" And I am walking. And then I see them again—it's the mob of Hollywood extras! They are taking furnitures from the store. And I tell myself, "I will need a bed to sleep in tonight." So I go get myself one...

I run inside and choose from a wide selection of merchandise. There is a sign: "CLEARANCE! EVERYTHING MUST GO!" Okay. I pick out my little mattress with tiny, heavenly angels drawn on it to remind me of my Catholic upbringing, and I set it up in the parking lot. But then I tell myself, "This is not enough for prosperous American lifestyle. I must have some more!" So I run in again, and again until I have my couch, my sofa chair, my beanbag, my love seat for the series of lovers I will meet in the United States once I start to lead openly gay lifestyle full of economic indulgence... Soon enough, I have an entire American living room! It is comfortable, Mamá. It is the most comfortable living room in the world. And America—my America—is one large living room, where anyone can steal his own couch! And to think, I already have it all in my first day in the United States of America.

But something is missing, Mamá, something else is missing in my new, prosperous lifestyle, now that I have everything. And that is a man. Can I go looting for a man? Well, that is exactly what I do! I break into the Porno Pleasure House on Santa Monica and find myself ten inches worth of a man, and I bring him into my living room, all ten inches of him staring me in the face—and I hold him in my arms—you always said I liked to play with dolls, Mamá... I have it all then, Mamá. I have a living room with a couch

Men on the Verge of a His-panic Breakdown

and coffee table and a rug and a ten-inch man in my hand. I am an American success. But all it takes is some pendejo with a cigarette lighter to set the couch on fire. And there it goes, Mamá, the couch first, then the lamp-table, the lamp, the bed, the rug, and then finally even the dildo is on fire! And there I stand, watching my American Dream go up in flames, and the looters gather around me and applaud, and tell me, "Welcome! Welcome to Los Angeles!" As the ten-inch dildo melts away into the night...

So you see, Mamacita, I write you this letter from the fire zone. With a piece of paper and pen I took from Thrifty. I write to you as the National Guard moves into my street—and I say, "Hello! Remember me? I'm Federico! You invaded my country a couple of years ago. I slept with a few of you." Men, how quickly they forget... So there they are again, bringing order back to the city. And we all return again to the life we had before... with twenty dollars in my pocket, a phone book full of wrong numbers, and the hope that the fires will die out and that I will find a place of my own to stay. A place to start again. And buy my first bed, my first couch, and my first man...

Good night, Mamacita. Your son, Federico.

(Lights fade out.)

SCENE TWO:

GOOD-BYE TO SUGAR DADDY

(VINNIE: youthful, pretty, but 30. Turning 30 is for him a crisis.)

He's 18?... No, no bother.

The point is well-taken, Sugar Daddy. Don't worry, it doesn't take me that long to pack. I can be out of here in a matter of minutes.

Now, if you could just sign here, and here, and down here... This form will help me seek compensation from the Society of West Hollywood Kept Boys Over 30...

Please, say no more. You'll be late for the Gay Republican fund-raiser.

I am *not* upset. Please. Let's be businesslike about this. And I'll leave a receipt for your taxes, yes...

Don't worry about me. I've been meaning to visit the folks back in Colombia, the ones who survived the last volcano eruption.

I've got all the bases covered. Self-reliant, independent, one-man show—that's me.

Men on the Verge of a His-panic Breakdown

Oh, I'll leave written instructions for the new 18-year-old from Wichita, Kansas, so he can deal with your prostate gland medicine.

You'll be late... Good-bye, Sugar Daddy.

(He watches Sugar Daddy go. A half-hearted wave good-bye... He's left alone. He looks around the room. He lights a cigarette. He makes a phone call.)

Hello, is this Lenny? Lenny, darling, how are you? Nice to hear your voice again after all these years. Why, it's Vinnie. Vinnie Contreras. Oh, come now... I was 20, you were 29. Ten years or so ago, remember?

I came in clutching Sugar Daddy's arm and we kindly asked you to depart from our presence. Yes, I helped you pack. But no, I don't remember throwing your bags out the window. Let memory be more selective, Lenny! Lenny?!?

So what have you been doing with your life? What? Oh, no particular reason, just wanted to keep in touch. No, no, it's not that at all—all right, Lenny, he's 18, he's blonde, fresh from Kansas. What am I to do, Lenny? Oh, oh, Lenny...

But please let me ask you, and I hope it's not too personal. What did you do after you voluntarily departed from Sugar Daddy's presence?... How many years at the shelter? I can't stand poor lighting, you know. But OK, afterwards, what did you do afterwards? Dry-cleaning? Oh, I love dry-cleaning, you know, I love the hangers and the plastic wrap that makes the clothes look so, you know, pressed! So, how

Men on the Verge of a His-panic Breakdown

much do they pay?... Oh, well, that's just slightly below the minimum wage... And no health care—well, that would be too Hillary, wouldn't it?

Listen, Lenny, do you think there might be an opening at the dry cleaners' any time soon? No, I just figured at this time in my life, I could use some...some flexibility. I'm exploring different venues for making a living. I'd like to be open to career alternatives... So, when do you think there might be an opening? Soon, you said? Oh, you didn't say.

Well, you'll keep me in mind, won't you, Lenny? Oh, no, no, Colombia is not for me these days, you know. I'm not sure if I belong at home at all, you know. No, I couldn't. I couldn't go back. I burnt too many bridges. Literally... Too many people tend to die when I burn bridges...

Lenny, wait! One more thing—

How did you ever feel about Sugar Daddy? You know, feelings. As in emotion? I know that about a half century separates me from him, but it can happen, right? Can it happen that after so many years, you can begin to feel a certain attachment to the creature? Oh, Lenny, there comes a time when even people like us develop feelings, don't you think?...

No, I'm *not*—I'm *not* crazy, Lenny.

After a while, you begin to develop feelings for those who pay your rent, feelings as noble and complex as any others.

Men on the Verge of a His-panic Breakdown

Feelings for his loose skin against your thighs, his dentures stuck in your pubic hair, his cancer-ridden lungs breathing sweet, warm air against your face.

Yes, Lenny, I love Sugar Daddy. I love Sugar Daddy! Only now do I realize it. Only now have I come to that conclusion.

Please don't. Don't hang up!... *(Desperate to keep him on the phone.)* We must get together for cappuccino at the Abby. Tea at Trumps? Attitude at the Studio? You no longer "do" attitude? Lenny!

(He hangs up the phone. He grabs his suitcase and holds it in his arms as a barrier against the world before him.)

Well, I suppose I understand why you had to hang up. I am alone now, ready to hit the streets. So here I go... I am one of the few, one of the brave, one of the Aging Kept Boys of West Hollywood.

I am not afraid. You hear that, world?

(As he "clicks his heels" three times.)

I am not afraid. I am not afraid. I AM NOT AFRAID!

(Lights fade out.)

SCENE THREE:

HISPANICALLY CORRECT

(EDWARD: a glamorous young man, mid-20s, California San Fernando Valley accent)

Hello... Is this, like, the Hispanic Hotline?

OK, this is my first time, you know. So, like, I'm supposed to give you the dirt and you're, like, supposed to tell me it's, like, Hispanically Correct. Is that right?

OK, so I'm, like, young and I'm, like, glamorous, OK? And when I first came to Hollywood a couple of years ago I, like, changed my name, I bleached my skin and I started frequenting the trendiest straight bars in town. My name now is, like, Edward Thornhill the Third. Well, never mind my real name. I can't even pronounce it, OK?

OK, so, like, recently this famous American movie actress whose name I couldn't possibly reveal—she, like, bought the rights to a well-known Mexican novel. And all of a sudden there was this wonderful part for, like, a Hispanic actor, OK? But my agent doesn't even know I'm, like, ethnic. And I have to sneak off to the audition all by myself and I'm really nervous, OK? But once I get there, I'm, like, really good, OK?

Men on the Verge of a His-panic Breakdown

I have a degree from Trish School of the Arts. No, not Tisch School of the Arts—but my friend Trish Lopez from East L.A. has this little studio where we learn our basic stereotypes, OK?...

So Rodge, the casting director for the movie, like, he comes up to me and he says, "Wow, we've never seen an Anglo do a Hispanic so good. How do you do it, kid?" And I tell him it comes naturally, OK?

So I come home, and I'm feeling really good, OK? I'm gonna sit by that phone, I'm gonna get that part, become a star and, like, I'm finally gonna have some friends, OK? So I come home, but who should be waiting at my doorstep?—

It's, like, Cynthia. She's this really gorgeous Greek goddess-type and all the agents love her because she's got the right name for the nineties: Cynthia Clintgore. That's her name, Cynthia Clintgore. So there she is, looking gorgeous in this lovely chiffon outfit that, you know, I'd love to borrow sometime.

And I make her come in, and I make her some tea. But she's not feeling too good. Her career isn't going anywhere—she can't act worth shit. So she goes on and on talking about her problems when all I want to do is, you know, talk about myself... So finally I lose my temper and I tell her, "Well, just tell me the story of your life, why don't you, Cynthia?" Not a good idea. She turns around and spits on the rug like a construction worker and she says she's really sick of me. She never meant to become my

Men on the Verge of a His-panic Breakdown

girlfriend. Nooo, her agent recommended it. And she says she isn't even an Anglo-Saxon Protestant from Omaha, Nebraska, like her press release says. No, instead, she's this bleached Latina, and is the chairwoman of the Closeted Minority Lesbian Union. And I'm, like, freaking out, OK?

And she says she knows everything about me and will expose me to the press unless I, Edward Thornhill the Third, give her, like, a baby. 'Cause she and her lesbian lover have been trying for years to conceive but I guess they can't, you know, because they're, like, members of the same sex and you need an egg and a sperm—oh, you know about that ... good.

So I tell her: "Hold on, Cynthia! You can go to a real good Nobel Prize-winning sperm bank and get a real good deal on an economist, OK?" And she says she doesn't want a genius, she wants a Hollywood actor. Because one day I, Edward Thornhill the Third, might get to become a star.

STAR! *Star*. There's something about that word that gets me really horny, you know?... So I tell her, "Let's go for it, Cynthia!"

So our bodies collide against each other like meteors and we land on the kitchen tile—and I feel like it's coming, this biblical act, this Genesis in the making, it's coming, IT'S COMING! When who should come walking into my apartment—

It's, like, my parents! They show up looking like real immigrants, you know? They were evicted from their East

Men on the Verge of a His-panic Breakdown

L.A. apartment because they're, like, poor and can't afford the rent—what a lame excuse! And they, like, come in and make themselves at home, drink up my fine Chablis and put on the Spanish channel. And, like, Cynthia wants to know when I'm going to get rid of these immigrants. And they want to know when I'm going to marry this bountiful Christian. They don't speak English. She doesn't speak Spanish. And I'm not about to translate, OK? When who should come walking into all of this—

It's, like, my agent! He's all excited because he got me a gig to play a clown at the annual Nancy and Ronnie Special Athletics for Retards. It's my agent's first fifteen percent commission. That's how pathetic he is. And he starts calling up his friends on my cordless phone. And soon, all these people start showing up at my doorstep. I don't know who they are, I don't know their names, and they don't even bring a picture and resume. And who should come walking into all of this, but Oh-My-God, it's like—

Rodge! The casting director of the movie that I tried out for. He stands there for the longest time and then he says, "Congratulations, kid! You're going to become a star!" But then he says, "And all you have to do is change your name to Hispanic."

"But, why?" I ask.

"Because," he says, "all these Hispanic activists will be upset if they find out an Anglo got a top Hispanic part. The only one for the year!"

Men on the Verge of a His-panic Breakdown

And I have to think on my feet. Think, think, think. Then I finally tell him, "OK, I'll change my name to Eduardo Troncos." And he says it doesn't sound Hispanic *enough* and I can't even tell the asshole it's my real name.

(Becoming frantic.) So he goes around the room asking people for better-sounding Hispanic names. And my agent wants to know what's going on, and Cynthia wants me to go into the bedroom to, like, fertilize her egg, and my parents are all upset because I made them wear these quaint little butler and maid uniforms—well, somebody had to pass out the hors d'oeuvres. And they're all calling: Eddie, Eddie, Eduardo, Eddie, Eduardo, Eddie, Eduardo!

And I finally snap and start shouting at all these people in this horrible high school Spanish— "Va fuera, va fuera, fuera!" And I start throwing things at the guests in what's turned into this sick little soiree! Dishes, lamps, copies of my resume and 8x10 glossies (it's always a good time to network), and my face snaps and all my plastic is hanging out, making me look more my age.

"Va fuera, va fuera!" I keep shouting, and the neighbor upstairs complains that I'm using the imperative interchangeably with the indicative! "This is no time for a grammar lesson, asshole! Fuera! Fuera!" And I chase everybody out the door, foaming at the mouth, and bang the door shut behind them all! *(Beat.)*

And what I'd really like to know, Hispanic Hotline: Is it, like, Hispanically Correct to, like, shut out the world and

Men on the Verge of a His-panic Breakdown

deny it all? Could I return to my real roots, my preformation as egg and sperm?

(He gets progressively more nervous, as they come to get him.)

I don't want to be connected to all this mess, all these rivalries between people like Mexican versus Anglo, English versus Spanish, woman versus man, gay versus straight, Armani versus Polo. Could I, like, become neutral to history itself and, like, make believe the Treaty of Guadalupe was just another crazy zoning law? Tell me it can be done, Hispanic Hotline! Give me a sign!

Oh my God! They're coming to get me, the foreigners, the Anglos, the lesbians, the Hollywood agents and producers! They're coming armed with nets and straitjackets, to take me away! Answer me, Hispanic Hotline! Don't cut me off now!

(Pantomimes being dragged away as he screams.)

HEEEEEEEEELP!

(Lights out.)

SCENE FOUR:

DEMON ROOMMATE FROM HELL

(Young man, lonely, asexual, living in Burbank by the airport.)

Well, here it is.

It's spacious, two-bedroom, quaint, airy, close to all the major freeways and yes, it's... *(As plane approaches.)* A LITTLE TOO CLOSE TO THE AIRPORT! BUT IT'S NOT *(Plane passes by.)* always this loud. You'll get used to it, and you can move in now, no deposit, no hidden fees, no problem! No, no catch. Just move in when you'd like and don't be shy about it. Do it now! No pressure, of course.

Look, I'll be perfectly honest with you. I like you! Your sincerity, your apprehension, your inability to grab a deal when you see one. It shows there's a lot about you that needs to be nurtured and reshaped if necessary. I really like that in a roommate! I can see you're out here from—what is it?—Tuscaloosa, Alabama! Southern, bubbly and blonde. And an actor, too, ready to conquer Burbank and its many pleasant environments! Why, I do declare! I'd like to be of help in your new surroundings.

Now, before you make any decisions, I'll put it all out on the table, just so it's out there—what else? The house rules,

Men on the Verge of a His-panic Breakdown

of course! First...no unwashed dishes, no dirty socks on the table, and no African bees! That's right, African bees! The last roommate used to leave the swing door open and you never know what can come in. And the African bees, you know they're coming, they've reached Texas, they're probably already here living in our midst without us even realizing it, but sooner or later, they'll strike, hundreds of them darkening the Burbank skies, buzzing and biting as hard as piranhas into your neck! So please, a simple rule, watch the swing door and be on the lookout always! They're out there!

The other thing...no genitals. The roommate before the last one used to walk around exposing himself in these tight underwear that he bought through the *International Male* catalogue, pure pornography that catalog, pure pornography! You pay $20 for a teeny piece of cloth that shows off your basket, and that thing is bound to pop out any time so I say—what? Smoking? Smoke all you like, just cover your damn genitals!

Which leads to the subject of guests, overnight or otherwise. I'm not that concerned with girlfriends or boyfriends or whatever, I don't care about that, and honestly I am looking for someone more like myself, sort of openly asexual which is very acceptable out here in Burbank, and my friends say I'm suffering from sexual repression, but I don't believe that's the case, some of us just don't have relationships, and that's OK. It's part of what it means to grow up and accept your limitations. So sex or no, you're welcome here, but I'm more concerned with...RELATIVES!

Men on the Verge of a His-panic Breakdown

I don't know about you, but relatives, my relatives, I wouldn't wish them upon any roommate, especially Dad, my dad, you know, after his experiences with the Chilean dictatorship, oh, that's all he ever talks about and he won't shut the hell up, the dictatorship this, the dictatorship that, we're such victims, he says, such victims, and I say, get over it already! But I won't get into it, the last roommate could tell you stories about relatives but—

What? What about the last roommate? Why did he leave? It's a very sensitive subject. Please don't force me to—it's a very doleful memory. You have a right not to know! Bu...all right. I suppose you can't make a decision without the facts. You have a right to know how the last roommate and I got along, why our relationship failed, and how he died!

No, please don't leave! Hear me out! Nobody ever hears me out! See what happens when people don't communicate! Surely back in Alabama, people sit down on the Porsche and talk over a glass of lemonade and a piece of sweet potato pahhh. OUT HERE IN BURBANK IT'S HARD TO TALK OVER THE PLANES, BUT it's not always this loud...

It happened very quickly that night when the roommate brought over a friend, "a friend"! Keep in mind the roommate was quiet, studious, bookish, all eager to sell that first screenplay over to Disney down the block. He wanted so badly to make it in Hollywood, but I noticed how he always wore this tight black turtleneck, corduroy pants, a wool scarf around his neck—this is Southern California! No shorts, no short sleeves for him. He was warm all right, but not to others, not to me at least. He barely greeted me when he came out of his room in the morning, and once for breakfast, he just reached over with half his grapefruit and smashed it against my face. He'd seen it in a James Cagney movie, he said. Oh, that's another rule, I prefer cold cereal—if I'm going to be trampled upon and abused by breakfast items, I prefer grains, no citrus fruits, please.

Anyway, he had never brought a friend over before and I must admit this friend was a beautiful young man— I don't use such words lightly, not for an asexual person, but I do recognize beauty when I see it, a tall young athlete in Olympic training no less. What he was doing here with Mr. Grapefruit Man, I'll never know!

So that's when Dad shows up to complicate things, and the roommate leaves for the bedroom with his friend because they don't want to hear about the Chilean dictatorship ... and Dad is going on and on about how unhappy he is, how grand his life used to be, all because he was big shit down there in Santiago, as the Head Torturer of political dissidents. He invented electric pliers and other methods of systematic pain, and now he just hates his new job as the head of the Burbank Dental Clinic. Nothing will ever be the same. But I'm barely listening to Dad, the roommate and the Olympian are alone in there, and I hear noises, intimate murmurs of systematic pleasure, or is it the mattress springs busting? I can't really tell, but my imagination works tremendously and vividly to conjure up images of grand man-to-man attachments, and deep in my heart, I'm feeling something alien to me: jealousy. And Dad is going on and on about how our lives will never be the same, we

Men on the Verge of a His-panic Breakdown

were respectable people of the torturing class, but the dictatorship ended and suddenly there was talk, talk of putting the torturers behind bars, and thank God, the great military heroes said no, you don't touch the ex-torturers or we'll stage another coup. So we go free, which doesn't stop the neighborhood people from picketing outside our home. *Torturadores*, they shouted, *Torturadores de mierda!* We had to leave, we had to go! Imagine being accused for doing your duty to the nation; for being patriotic, family-oriented people! Only Disney would have understood!

But Dad won't shut up about it now and so that day I finally tell him: I don't care any more, Daaad, I don't care if we're no longer the leading torture family of Santiago, I don't care if we never go back, I have a life right here in sunny little Burbank! Dad slaps me hard on the face as he did to Mom and Grandma, and I go rolling over my precious pots of bougainvilleas in bloom...the stems are crushed, the pots shattered. Satisfied, Dad leaves it at that and returns to his dental clinic where he'll do the most damage with people's nerves.

So I'm left here all alone with the roommate and the Olympian inside...and I'm scared, scared of what I might do. I try to freshen up, pour myself a glass of my wondrous mineral water. I buy it by the gallons, I keep it fresh, fresh in the refrigerator, and I feel the glaze of a fresh gallon bottle against my skin, and that's when I finally realized—the boys need this more than I do!

So I break through the door and I see them both on the bed, one of them with his shirt off, and I pour the entire gallon

Men on the Verge of a His-panic Breakdown

of fresh, iced water on their firm, naked bodies. *(Attacks like Psycho killer.)* Time to cool it, cool it, cool it!

And that's how the roommate died...death by mineral water! Pneumonia actually! The police were rather gentle on me, figuring how was I supposed to know that the young man suffered from an unusual condition that kept his body temperature low, that's why he always wore turtlenecks and scarves...and the young Olympian was one of his trainers, or so he said, who helped him, you know, warm up. I was not charged with anything. Another screenwriter is dead in Burbank and nobody asks the hard questions! The Olympian beauty is gone to train in Atlanta and I am here eager to start again. I desperately need a roommate!

So...the first three months are free, and I can throw in free cooking of Chilean food and long nights of laid-back conversation to remind you of your rustic life in good ole Dixie. Where did you go? Mr. Alabama? Mr. Ala— *(The phone rings.)* Hello... Yes, the room is still available. Full of charm, ambience, airy! Would you like to come by tomorrow? Yes, it's near all the studios AND THE AIRPORT IS A BIT TOO CLOSE BUT IT'S NOT ALWAYS THIS LOUD! *(Ominous tone of voice.)* You'll get used to it

(Lights down. An intermission may be taken here, if desired.)

SCENE FIVE

FEDERICO WRITES AGAIN

(In the shadow, we see FEDERICO wearing a Streisand wig and doing a sign-language interpretation of "People Who Need People" while the music plays. He takes off the wig, and approaches a block or a chair where he begins his second letter.)

Querida Madre,
Dear Mother,

The excitement of the California lifestyle continues.

I got my first job catering the homes of Topanga Canyon—and in my first day of work—all the houses burn down... I rescue a Labrador, and the police declare me a hero. They take my picture and give me a five-dollar reward—and then they call the INS, so I have to go running... But they give me five minutes head start to run—because I'm a hero!

And finally I meet somebody who likes me, Mamá! You know what I mean... in the romantic department. He's a deaf impersonator who does Barbra Streisand in sign language. Joey's a blond boy from Kentucky, and he knows some Spanish sign language too—but I know no sign in any language—and he has to teach me from scratch, and that way he doesn't have to listen to my accent, but I feel

Men on the Verge of a His-panic Breakdown

like I have an accent in sign language too! My hands mispronounce everything—ay que clumsy!

He take me to live with him in his Northridge apartment, and we move there on January 16, 1994. We stay up all night just signing away and talking about our lives, and we go to bed all snuggled up against each other... And at 4:31 a.m. the building SHAKES and all the Streisand wigs go flying out the window!

And he's all shook up, and in the dark a deaf person can't exactly sign for help, can he?... But he's BLEEDING, so I take him to the nearest hospital—and with my bad English and his sign language, nobody understands what we have to say...

Until some nasty nurse tells him he has no health insurance, and that he should go back to his own country—and she thinks he's an illegal alien just because he speak sign language!

Until finally a doctor come to help us. He take out pieces of broken glass from Joey's toes and then stitch him up.

But then he take a good look at me, and I feel the piercing wounds of arrows! He's a handsome, tall Irish man—and his eyes reveal the sadness of someone who is successful at everything else except, you know, in the romantic department.

He feel sorry for us, true, but more than anything else, he feel sorry for himself. He has no lover... So he take us both to live with HIM!

And for several months, we both become the doctor's assistants, and we live in Bel Air!... Our job was to feed the Abyssinian cats and keep our bodies tanned. We do the dishes by day, and by night we clear the cobwebs of the doctor's private life—if you know what I mean, Mamacita. No more details—I'm blushing!

But one day, the doctor decide to run for Congress, and with tears in his eyes, he ask us to go... Because the press is asking too many questions about his houseguests, and he want to declare his opposition to illegal aliens *and* deaf people...

So Joey and me walk the streets of Los Angeles again, and we wonder where our next job will come from... Who need another sign language Streisand imitator?... Who need another immigrant?...

I write this letter from the park overlooking the shelter, with stationery I take from the doctor...

Isn't that the American way of life, Mamá? Los Angeles is the one place where nature forces you to start again and again—and so the excitement continues! Only in America, Mamá! Only in America!

(Lights fade out.)

SCENE SIX:

CASTRO'S QUEEN

(PACO: a middle-aged man with a guayabera and cigar.)

You'll ruin me, you immigrants! I'm not gone for three days and the place looks like the aftermath of unos quinces—you know, a debutante ball turned into an orgy! Not even a good one!

Last night on my way home from the airport, I drove by just to check things out from a distance, and what do I find? That my marquee is off, at 9 o'clock at night, my marquee is off! How are people going to be enticed into Paco's Cuban Restaurant—an Oasis in the Phoenix Culinary Desert?

I drove home with tears clouding my vision. I drove into a cactus. My body is still prickled all over. *(Picks off a needle from his rear end.)*

And talk about cacti! I'll have you know my friend Butch Lupe, *she* dropped by last night to check things out and guess what she found in my Pollo a la Cienfueguesa—a slice of nopal! Mamá's favorite recipe for chicken in yucca sauce cannot be substituted with nopal! Yucca has its own integrity! One does not mess with yucca.

Men on the Verge of a His-panic Breakdown

What would I do without my lesbian friends to spy for me?! I'm gone for three days to my *Palm Springs Workshop for Entrepreneurial Homosexuals Abandoned by Their Loved Ones Bearing the Full Weight of the Universe*, and *this* is what I find?

You're out to destroy me! You Mexicans are all on Castro's payroll. From the chef down to the busboys, what we have here is one giant communist conspiracy of incompetence!

I know we're understaffed, but I provide a decent work environment once the Prozac kicks in, don't I?... I'll tell you right now: bankruptcy is in the air, and I won't have us lose our jobs on account of one missing piece of yucca... We must not betray the cause of Caribbean cuisine.

Where is your work ethic? At your age, I was serving up a storm of ropa vieja and arroz con pollo at my father's restaurant, La Habana de Noche! I was the owner's son, yet I was not above cleaning tables and emptying trash cans.

Even when the revolution came and Dad insisted on leaving, I said, "You do that, but I will serve the revolution. I will bring fine food to the masses!" I believed in the revolution then, I was a convert.

But then Castro decided to round up all of us queers, and put us in concentration camps. Los campamentos UMAP. We were undesirables. And did I give up *then*? No, I found a way to serve my fellow inmates with a sense of decorum. Tin plates, mushy beans and rice, our hands used as nap-

Men on the Verge of a His-panic Breakdown

kins? NO! I developed *concentration-camp etiquette*. Castro tried to make us act and eat like the straight man—with our hands; they wanted us to belch out loud—but I made sure my boys burped quietly and cleaned the tip of their lips on cloth napkins that I, myself, embroidered out of rags, with little palm tree figures and everything.

I was determined to keep alive the flame that El Viejo, Papi, had proudly set up at la Habana. In the end, we the Cuban queers, were just dropped on these shores like refuse. The revolution decided we were hopeless. That they could never turn etiquette-minded queers like me into straight revolutionary communists. They put us on a boat to Florida during the Mariel Boat Lift, and we thought our troubles were over.

I thought El Viejo would welcome me and put me to work in his Miami diner, "El Criollo Loco." But it turns out Papi was ashamed that I was in "those camps," not just your average concentration camps for political dissidents, but "those camps" for undesirables, like me. I was the only point on which my father agreed with the revolution.

Even in Miami, he said I'd become too obvious. That I'd been much more discreet before. Papi said he'd invest in some business elsewhere, a booming business town, somewhere far away, perhaps I could go away and colonize the desert.

He put the down payment for Paco's Cuban Restaurant, and the rest was up to me. There wasn't enough of a down payment for West Hollywood, or the Village, or the Castro

Men on the Verge of a His-panic Breakdown

District—somebody should change that name—but anyway, the investment was good enough for Phoenix. El Viejo doesn't want me back. I'm not invited to family get-togethers. And it doesn't matter that I've had a few years of prosperity, and it doesn't even matter that I'm the president of Arizona Gay Republicans. El Viejo does not call or write.

And then—there's that Carlos' Havana Room opening by city hall. Carlos owns *chains* of Havana Rooms! He's a Cuban-American princess, *y casi ni habla español*, Americanized piece of shit! *Come mierda!* He's young, has a well-toned body, and I hear he's even in a long-term relationship!

But there's only room for one Cuban faggot restaurateur in all of Phoenix! And that's me, Paco!... So, you see, our jobs depend on battling this enemy, which is no longer communism, but the indifference of the universe, the indifference of the desert.

So... it's up to you to share my dream. It's up to you to get your shit together and push this dream forward. One day you'll be in my shoes, prospering and aging just as gracefully as I'm doing, and leaving the marquee on, and making sure el Pollo a la Cienfueguesa is not polluted by nopal!

So, shall we? I mean, you need the jobs, and I might be able to afford a raise when we pull through... You *will* stay with me, won't you? After all, I *need* you... I meant to say that a long time ago...

You will stay?... Of course you will. Who else would listen to me like this?

Oh... Oh my God! Here they come! Put on the sash, Miguel. Busboys, man your stations and hold the water jugs up high with the pride of a true Cubano. Chef, back to the kitchen, and please, don't ignore the yucca!

Here they come, with their ominous-looking briefcases. Is it the lunch crowd, or an army of debt collectors? *(He laughs feebly at his attempt at a joke.)* We'll find out soon, won't we? As we push forward in this risky world of freedom, in this wondrous enterprise known as Paco's Cuban Restaurant—an Oasis in the Phoenix Culinary Desert.

Welcome! So glad you could make it! We like you!...

(Fade to black.)

SCENE SEVEN:

ESL: ENGLISH AS A STRESSFUL LANGUAGE

(Young Latino male, early 30s—but looks older. A prime candidate for a transcultural shock, otherwise known as a His-panic breakdown. His tone is too happy, as if talking down to children. He's nervous, and totes a handkerchief which he uses to continuously wipe his brow.)

Good morning, my little immigrants. We are here to learn the English language. *(Beat.)*

I SAID... *(Enunciating.)* We are here to learn the English language brought to you by the pilgrims. English... Don't leave home without it.

Now, this is not a simple language. None of that Romance language kid stuff—none of that one sound per every vowel. No, in this language you are allowed to make dozens of sounds per each vowel. There's no point in worrying about it—you'll never get it right. Because when it comes to pronunciation, English is a mind-fuck. Repeat after me: English is a mind-fuck.

Feel free to practice... Practice makes perfecto! Ooops!

(Spanish slipped out. He looks a bit self-conscious.)

Men on the Verge of a His-panic Breakdown

While you do that, I'll tell you a little bit about myself. I was born in a house "my father built with his own hands," to quote my hero the late Richard Nixon. *(Wipes a tear.)* Dad was a farmer. Yes, we were poor...except, of course, when the coca leaves flourished in the spring. We came to America to evade the U.S. Army, if you get my drift, compadre—oops. Excuse me.

It's true, then. English is my second language, but it rolled me into its bosom like the mother tongue. It became my predominant language, you might say, overnight. It wooed me into its winning ways and winnowed me out, separating the wheat from the weaker chaff among wou—you.

And that's how I became an ESL instructor. Well, I didn't get accepted into art school, but that's all right. Neither did Hitler. No, instead, I ended up sharing my wisdom with a bunch of foreigners who remind me too much of my parents and who'll never learn the language of Princess Di.

So, what's *your* excuse, Maria? Cat got your tongue? You've been sitting there for the past five years. I've seen you grow into an old woman. Along the way, you've given birth to six, seven welfare children. For five years, you have failed to memorize the past participle, let alone the present perfect, the past perfect and the present perfect continuous. And you can forget the future perfect or the future perfect continuous, as in: "Tomorrow I *will have <u>learned</u>*" but the future never quite arrives, does it? Although tomorrow, you probably "*will have <u>conceived</u>*" yet again... Oh, you say the job at the sewing factory wears you down, seventy hours a week and only a few hours left at night for the

Men on the Verge of a His-panic Breakdown

study of this foreign, so very foreign language— I've heard all the excuses, and the truth is, the truth is...your Spanish stinks just as badly... I would fail you in your own language, but I can't, I'm only the English teacher. If I were the Spanish teacher, there'd be blood on the table. *(He breaks.)* SANGRE!—oops.

Now you, you, Julio. The one with the tight jeans. Yes, I've noticed how much tighter they've gotten through the years. I bet you're in love with the teacher, too. One day, we will communicate, you and I. We will break the silence. I will leave my marriage of convenience to that assembly senator's daughter from Orange County. And you, you, Julio, will be there as my receptacle of desire... Yes, I've seen you with Lucita, that Salvadoran girl you picked up at La Taverna Manusiosa. I've seen her waiting for you after class, holding a tray of tortitas and pupusitas, and all that Salvadoran fast-food stuff. I've seen you devour her food out there by the picnic table. Will you ever devour my homemade Paella a la Sevillana? Why not? Hey, I hang out with women myself. I married one. I am very comfortable with my sexual repression... But I am fortunate, at least, in that I can sodomize you with my words and bend you over without lubricants—and you don't understand a word I'm saying!

One day, we will communicate. See things eye to eye... We will rise from the earth, and, ah...

What? Hunh? Who interrupted the teacher in his lustful soliloquy? Was it you, Mr. Campos? Another one of your runs to the bathroom? Seventy-five years old and pretending to learn English as a second language, when the truth is, the dirty truth is...you come here for company! Company! As in human touch, consideration, to get away from all those monolingual grandchildren who refuse to speak Spanish with you. But how am I supposed to help you? When that last stroke wiped out the past tense, including my favorite, the past perfect continuous.

Here, in my classroom, you grunt, you aahh, you oohh, you grumble, as your head bobs up and down, up and down. Now is *this* learning, Mr. Campos? At your age, I would have given up. But you, Mr. Campos, you *insist*, you will fight to the bitter end. I disdain heroism, Mr. Campos, that's why I teach grammar! So to answer your question: "No, you may not go to the bathroom until you learn to raise your hand and ask in perfect Chaucerian English." SO HOLD IT!

And you, Mrs. Rosales, sweet little Mrs. Rosales, who came out of nowhere one night and has sat there ever since. We don't know if you're Mexican or Salvadoran or Guatemalan. The combination of Spanish and English has blown a fuse in your wee little brain, and you can no longer speak any language whatsoever. You sit there, you wickedly smile and you point—what are you pointing at? Are you pointing at me by any chance? Please, do not point at me. I didn't do it. Whatever it is I'm guilty of, I'm not guilty of it. I'm only doing my job...

What? For some odd reason, Mrs. Rosales has chosen today to point at the Statue of Liberty... Oohhh, I'm very proud of you, Mrs. Rosales. We welcome your downtrodden sentimentality. *(Wipes a tear.)*

As you know, I care about you all. I care about you, you, you, and *(To Julio.)* I definitely care about you, sugar buns. You are all my future fellow citizens, and I must have a job to survive in these downsizing times. For better or for worse, I am one of you, and we are stuck with each other, aren't we? We may succeed, or most probably fail, but we'll do it together!

The past tense of "eat shit"? Look it up in the dictionary.

All right, let's get to work! Mr. Campos, empty out your piss-pot in the cacti. Maria, wake up or you'll conceive in your sleep. You, hot buns, smile at me from the *other* end. One day, we *will* make sense to one another. One day, the horizon will open, the clouds will roll away, and we will communicate. We will stand as one, and we shall all speak English!

And by then, we'll all have to learn Japanese.

(Lights fade out.)

SCENE EIGHT:

DRAG FLAMENCO

(LA GITANA: a young man dying of AIDS. He is sitting on a hospital bed. As the monologue progresses, he dons a flamenco dress, a wig, and some drag make-up.)

How grand? How fabulous can one be in one's own deathbed?

La Gitana, they call me. Oh, I've been called by many names before—the obvious ones: faggot, queer, puta, maricona, trash, tramp, loca, mariposa, fairy, mamona, sinverguenza, perdida, asquerosa, bella y muy tramposa. But only one of them stuck.

La Gitana, they call me... after the gypsy blood in me mixed with the Moorish Andalusian strains in my precious, delicate veins that have sustained generations of my kind. And we have survived and thrived and grown to be grand and esplendida!... And now La Gitana is back... not the roundish little gordita that she used to be, a little wan perhaps, a little feint and delicate. If you'd been abandoned by both your lover and your T-cells, you'd look a little weary yourself—no crees, mi reina?

Men on the Verge of a His-panic Breakdown

She is ready now to take her place among the immortals. "Bring me the castanets," she insists, "they'll cover some of the lesions on the hands!"

She prepares to stand again in the spotlight among her fans—men that paid for her flamenco fire on their chests. Men who once used her and abused her, maybe even loved her. They're here now and she demands respect— Mas respeto, chico, eh?! And then there's rumors that *he'll* be here tonight to witness the act. You know, *he*.

He who brought her to the U.S. from Fuentevaqueros, Spain. Desolate land of poets. Ay, mi Fuentevaqueros... He lured her away from her magic homeland of dance and poetry. She lithped her way across the continent like a good Spanish girl until the two made a home in Los Angeles, part of the old kingdom once. She felt right at home!

At first she was a stripper, they say. Her man—the one with the slicked back "do" and the open shirt and chains around his chest—learned early the marketing of she. Her. La Gitana. He understood that her talents, her passion, unraveled themselves in her wrists, in the movements of castanets like little tremors of Southern California earth, and then in her heels, the blood sent from the fists down to the little delicate toes, creating a forceful collision with the earth until sparks flew and the old kingdom of España was on fire in her veins... It came naturally to her, she was—

(She coughs, unable to finish the sentence.)

Men on the Verge of a His-panic Breakdown

And yes, she loved him. Rather she felt drawn to him as some are to a drug all too powerful to resist, a habit impossible to break. Hers was the love of criminals, the love of blood and passion, de fuego y de polvora, de muerte y de vida!

Soon, she became in demand. La Gitana would do the castanets and the "zapateo" for you and weave herself into the fabric of your soul.

And he, he was there to take his ten percent, which mounted to twenty, thirty, and forty percent if you take into account the coke she bought for him on the road, by train, by bus, by plane.

And once in Washington state, she found herself a closeted apple picker. Family man with ten children, all lonely in the bar holding his Miller Draft. He begged her to stay in Washington, but the other "he," you know, the man with the "do," confronted the sweaty, sensual apple picker. Threatened him with exposing his secret among the apple grapevines— Someone pulled a knife, and La Gitana had to expose her false titties to the blade of the knife, coming between the men to break up the fight.

Oh, after a while he only wanted her to dance for him alone, and it became obvious that *she* had a "he" problem. That he would eventually ruin her career, that he would ruin her reputation as a reputable tramp and she would no longer be welcomed anywhere. But she told the world, "He comes with me or I don't perform." And so the nightclub

Men on the Verge of a His-panic Breakdown

owners tolerated him, because La Gitana would not have it any other way.

And the day came when, like so many other young men around her, she became ill. La Gitana could no longer continue to dance as she once did. She could no longer pay her electrolysis bills, let alone health care. But he... Oh, he was nowhere to be found! The day after her diagnosis was revealed, he went traveling again. The entire women's chorus of Bulgaria is now said to be his discovery—it's filled with drag queens!

For months she has languished in this hospital bed... For months she has hoped for his return.

Tonight, my friends, La Gitana has thought to herself, "Fuck him," and returned to you instead. You, the adoring public. You, who've held firm for the return of... *(Coughs.)*

They said it couldn't be done. Why couldn't she just stay in her hospital room? Why couldn't she just take her AZT with Zima and sleep tonight? No, instead, La Gitana *insists*—as her ancestors did—to perform until that final moment, that grand moment when the last breath passes through her ruby red lips. She's a stubborn one, this gypsy tramp, esta puta gitana asquerosa y muy tramposa! Y ya está qui—in her sold-out performance. There will be no extensions...

She will look around at her adoring public, and then she will say:

"Thank you, thank you. I am La Gitana, and tonight I will dance for you, and I will dance for the thousands who no longer dance among us. And I will dance for that empty chair that symbolizes 'him,' he who has no excuses for his absence... Allow me this final breath—this final indulgence so that I might live eternally, so that I might love and be loved again.

"As I deserve it. For I am the Spanish pearl of Fuentevaqueros. I am the treasure that washed unto these shores. A blast from the past. The Spanish jewel blazing deep in the soul of old California. I am the daughter of Andalusian Moors, princess of old Arabian nights, cousin of the great sensual poets whom I will join upon my demise.

"I am La Gitana!"

And for you, my gran "ZAPATEO!"

(She warms up to a loud gypsy yell as she dances her life away. Lights fade out.)

EPILOGUE

THE MARRIAGE OF FEDERICO

(Sound of fireworks to evoke the feeling of Independence Day. FEDERICO, the gay little immigrant, returns carrying a bag of oranges.)

Knock, knock, knock... Hello, it's me... I'm back... Remember me?... I'm Federico.

Last year, you refused to open the door for me. Well, I'm still around—and I haven't forgotten you, pendejo!

Hello! I know you're in there!

You come to my country and make all these promises, and then I come here and you threaten to call the INS, the L.A.P.D., and the NEA.

Look, I'm not going to go away just like that. There's millions of immigrants behind me and they're all coming here sooner or later... There is no place to hide.

Look, let me tell you—I am married now!

After you so rudely shut the door on me during the L.A. riots, I meet Joey in time for the quake. And after we're evicted from the congressman's house, we meet Dyke Di-

Men on the Verge of a His-panic Breakdown

ana and her Brazilian girlfriend, Lucita, in Van Nuys, looking for two queer roommates who don't mind putting up with Strictly Messy Lesbians.

So we start talking and we realize that Lucita is in this country without papers, and so am I. But since gay couples can't get married in America—in defense of marriage—we get a brilliant idea. Dyke Diana proposes to me, and Deaf Joey proposes to Lucita, and we are all married in one big wedding in Presbyterian church.

But the INS comes calling one night to check out if we really *are* couples, and... It's 4 a.m., and they're banging on the door. I wake up Joey, and in the dark, I run out and shout at Dyke Diana and Lucita to come exchange partners... So we all make this big switch, and take our family pictures and clothes and other personal belongings. I go back to my bed, and get ready to say "Come in" to the INS officers—when suddenly I notice—I'M IN BED WITH THE WRONG LESBIAN!

We scream and go dashing out the door to switch again until we get it right. Dyke Diana in my bed, Joey in Lucita's bed... But the closeness and the intimacy prove too much for Joey and Lucita who harbor bisexual tendencies, so they end up making love just as the INS agents come barging in in the middle of heterosexual intercourse! The INS agents are satisfied that these are real, straight, all-American couples, and they *approve our papers*.

So now Lucita is pregnant with Joey's child and we're all going to raise a beautiful kid with two mommies and two

Men on the Verge of a His-panic Breakdown

daddies. We'll teach him English, Spanish, Portuguese and sign language.

So, you see, I'm not obsessed with you opening the door and talking to me again—you "first love" you—pendejo de mierda!

No. I am married now. I am legal. And soon I stop selling oranges by the freeway and move up to minimum wage job at Fatty Burger's.

I survive whether you help me or not, and whether you like it or not, and whether I'm legal or not.

(Picks up an American Flag, the last item on the set. Fireworks.)

I am an immigrant. I am the future of this great country of ours. They call me Federico, The Gay Little Immigrant That Could.

I am an American success. I'm here to stay...so...get used to it.

THE END

DIRECTOR'S NOTES

DIRECTOR'S NOTES

DIRECTOR'S NOTES

DIRECTOR'S NOTES

DIRECTOR'S NOTES

DIRECTOR'S NOTES

DIRECTOR'S NOTES